MUSICAL INSTRUMENTS

Alan Blackwood

The Bookwright Press
New York · 1987

Topics

The Age of Dinosaurs
Airports
Ancient Peoples
Archaeology
Bridges
Castles
Costumes and Clothes
Earthquakes and Volcanoes
Energy
Farm Animals
Fairs and Circuses
Ghosts and the Supernatural
Great Disasters
Helicopters
Houses and Homes

Inventions
Jungles
Maps and Globes
Money
Musical Instruments
Peoples of the World
Photography
Pollution and Conservation
Prisons and Punishments
Robots
Spacecraft
Television
Trees of the World
Under the Ground
Zoos

First published in the
United States in 1987 by
The Bookwright Press
387 Park Avenue South
New York, NY 10016

ISBN 0–531–18146–4

Library of Congress Catalog Card Number: 87–70040

First published in 1987 by
Wayland (Publishers) Ltd
61 Western Road, Hove
East Sussex BN3 1JD, England

© Copyright 1987 Wayland (Publishers) Ltd

Phototypeset by
Kalligraphics Ltd, Redhill, Surrey
Printed in Belgium by
Casterman sa, Tournai

All the words that appear
in **bold** are explained in the
glossary on page 30.

Contents

How Musical Sounds are Made   4

Stringed Instruments   7

Wind Instruments   12

Percussion Instruments   20

Keyboard Instruments   24

Electronic Instruments   27

Glossary   30

Books to Read   31

Index   32

How Musical Sounds are Made

Our prehistoric ancestors made musical instruments with the natural objects that they found around them.

In prehistoric times, people made musical instruments out of various natural objects that they came across. They found large sea shells (conch shells), or hollowed-out rams' horns, that they could blow

into. Pieces of bone were sometimes made into pipes, or into drumsticks, and stones were made into rattles. What our ancestors were doing was creating vibrations or **sound waves** in the air. These reach our ears as actual sounds.

The most important aspect of musical sounds is their **pitch** – whether they are high-sounding or low-sounding notes. The pitch of a note depends on the rate or **frequency** of its vibrations. The faster (or the higher) the frequency of the vibrations, the higher will be the pitch of the sound we hear. (Try experimenting with an elastic band or piece of string. As you pull it tighter it will vibrate faster when you twang it, and the sound you hear will become higher-pitched.) The Greek philosopher Pythagoras was fascinated by this scientific fact. He believed the entire universe – sun, moon, planets, stars – moved according to special

The Greek mathematician Pythagoras was one of the first people to relate musical sounds to mathematics.

A jazz band in New Orleans. The musicians are playing trumpet, double bass, piano, clarinet, banjo and drums. Each of these instruments has a quality of sound unique to itself.

vibrations or frequencies, which he called "The Music of the Spheres."

Musical sounds also have their own special **tone** or quality. It is this question of tone that, for example, always makes the sound of a trumpet quite different from that of a violin, even when the two instruments are playing notes of exactly the same pitch.

Stringed Instruments

There are many pictures in old books and manuscripts, and in stained-glass windows in churches, of King David playing the harp. He was the most famous musician of ancient times, and the harp is one of the oldest of stringed

Harps are among the oldest instruments. There are many different sizes ranging from the hand-held harp played by King David to the modern concert type shown here.

The violin has a very wide range of pitched notes. The violinist in the picture is "stopping" the strings with her left hand.

instruments. Each string is tightened across the frame to a different degree, or is a different length, so that each vibrates at its own frequency and sounds its own note when plucked.

A violin has only four strings, each stretched and **tuned** to sound a different note. But violinists can press their fingers down on the strings, where they are stretched along the "neck" of the instrument. This stops part of the pressed string from vibrating and thus changes the pitch of the note. The technique is called "stopping." Violinists also rub or scrape the strings with a **bow**. This keeps them vibrating and sounding a note for a far longer time than the plucked strings of a harp, for instance. Violas, cellos and double basses belong to the violin "family" of instruments. With longer, thicker strings, and larger wooden frames, they sound notes of a lower pitch.

The string section of the Vancouver Symphony Orchestra of Canada – the cellos and double basses are on the right and the violins and violas on the left.

Niccolo Paganini was one of the first virtuoso musicians – someone who astonished everybody with his amazing technique. He also composed music.

The most famous violin maker was Antonio Stradivari, who worked with other fine craftsmen in Italy, about three hundred years ago. Violins made by him are today worth many thousands of dollars. One of the most celebrated of all violinists was another Italian, Niccolo Paganini. He was a very tall, thin, strange-looking man, and because he could play in such an amazing way, people said be must have sold his soul to the Devil!

Some other instruments have strings that are plucked, like those of a harp, but are also "stopped," like those of a violin. The guitar is one of these. The old Spanish or classical guitar is quite different from the modern electric guitar, which we shall look at on page 27.

The Spanish or classical guitar is played for flamenco singing and dancing – the traditional music of Spain. It is one of the most exciting instruments when played by experts.

Wind Instruments

To sound a conch shell or a ram's horn, you have to press or purse the lips against one end and blow hard. This produces sound waves inside the shell or horn. Brass wind instruments – called by this name because many of them are made of brass – are played in this way. Old-fashioned brass instruments were just long tubes – either straight or coiled – and because they could

A native of Peru making music by blowing into a conch shell. Notice how hard he is having to blow!

A Swiss alpine horn, traditionally used for signaling across mountain valleys. In other mountainous countries such as Tibet, even bigger and louder horns are used.

make a loud noise, they were useful for giving signals. Soldiers used bugles and trumpets to sound battle calls, such as "advance" or "retreat." Huntsmen blew on their horns to call to each other as they galloped on horseback over the countryside. In Switzerland and Tibet enormous instruments, like horns, were used to send signals across the mountains.

Modern brass instruments – such as trumpets, horns, trombones and tubas – have a small, cup-shaped mouthpiece at one end, to fit the player's lips. It is called the **embouchure**. This makes them easier to play and improves their tone. The other end widens right out, to give even more richness of tone to the sound, and is called the bell. Modern trumpets and horns also have valves, which the player presses down or releases, to alter the length of the tube. Trombones have a section of tube that slides in and out, like a piston. By using these methods, more notes can be played.

A large modern jazz band consists mainly of wind instruments. In the picture we can see, from left to right, saxaphones, trombones and trumpets.

Other wind instruments do not need to be blown so hard. In some cases, the player blows quite gently across one end of a pipe, or across an opening in it (also called an embouchure), to create sound waves inside. This is how recorders and flutes are played. In the case of oboes, clarinets and bassoons, the player blows onto a thin vibrating **reed**. Such instruments are called woodwinds, because traditionally they were all made of wood.

James Galway, the famous Irish musician, playing the modern transverse flute – one that the player holds at an angle to his mouth. Notice the keys he is operating.

One of London's famous military bands on parade. The bandsman closest to us is playing a euphonium – a special type of tuba. Behind him are cornets and horns.

A very old type of woodwind instrument was the pan pipes, which had a separate pipe for each note. All the other woodwinds have one tube or pipe only, with holes along the side, which the player covers or uncovers to sound different notes. With old instruments, players used their fingers to cover the holes but they often found it difficult to stretch their fingers so far. So a German flute player called Theobald Boehm designed a new type of instrument, with little **keys** and levers that operated the opening and closing of the holes. Most woodwind instruments are now made according to his designs.

A Peruvian playing an ancient version of the pan pipes. You can see that there is a pipe of different length for each note.

The Scottish pipes are the most famous type of bagpipe today, but bagpipes of other varieties have been played in many parts of the world.

One type of wind instrument unlike any other, is the bagpipes. The piper first blows a supply, or reservoir, of air into a kind of bag or sack, then squeezes it with his elbow, forcing air into the pipes. By keeping up the flow of air to the pipes he is able to produce a characteristic droning sound.

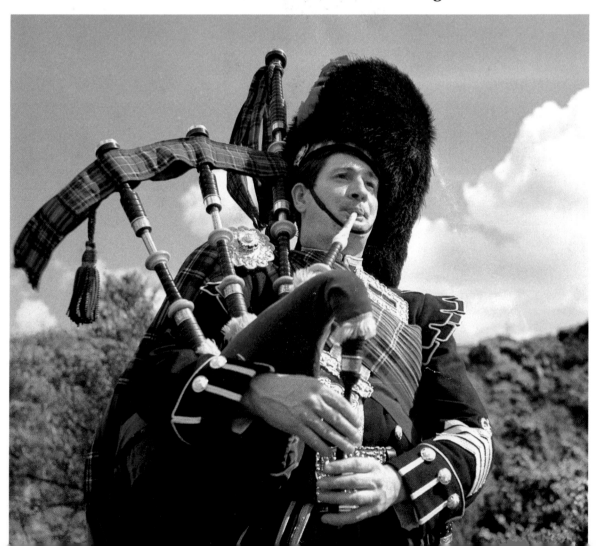

A modern saxophone player, or saxophonist. Saxophones are made in several different sizes, each producing its own range of notes.

A much more up-to-date instrument, but also in a class of its own, is the saxophone. It has a reed, and keys and levers to operate the holes, but is made of brass or some other metal, and has a bell-shaped end. So it is a cross between woodwind and brass. Its inventor, Adolphe Sax, thought his saxophones would sound good in military bands, but today they are mostly played in jazz bands.

Percussion Instruments

Long ago, hunters and warriors used to stretch the dried skin of a dead animal, or of some enemy killed in battle, across the top of a bowl or pot. Beating the skin made it vibrate, and produced a buildup of sound waves inside the pot. Such drums were sacred, since it was believed they recalled the spirit of

African tribal drums. Such drums, like old wind instruments, were often used to send messages from one village to the next.

the dead beast or person whose skin they were made from.

Drums and all other instruments that are played by hitting or striking them to create sound waves are called percussion instruments. They come in many shapes and sizes. Gongs and cymbals are flattened-out metal discs.

The drums of the famous West Indian steel bands are made from the tops of oil drums. These have been hammered into shapes that produce different musical notes.

An unusual xylophone band. The players are wearing their instruments strapped around their necks.

Xylophones consist of a row of wooden bars or blocks of different sizes, each sounding a different note when struck. Then there are bells, ranging from small tinkling handbells, to huge ones weighing many tons. These may be struck from the outside by a hammer, or have a "clapper" that strikes the inside of the bell as it swings from side to side.

Pop groups and jazz bands usually have a great many drums and cymbals. The percussion section of a modern orchestra is even bigger. Besides kettledrums, there are side drums, bass drums, gongs, cymbals, triangles, tubular bells, a xylophone, a glockenspiel, tambourines, clappers, wooden blocks and rattles. The percussion section is often called the "kitchen sink department" of the orchestra. because it seems to include everything but the kitchen sink!

Kettledrums (or timpani) and cymbals belong to the percussion section of an orchestra.

Keyboard Instruments

These are instruments with a row of keys or levers – the keyboard – that the player presses down, one for each note to be played. One old type of keyboard instrument is the harpsichord. It has a set of strings arranged much like those of a harp. The player presses the various keys, operating a mechanism that plucks the strings.

About the year 1710, an Italian craftsman, Bartolomeo Cristofori, invented a new kind of keyboard mechanism, which struck the strings with little hammers, instead of plucking them. He proudly called his new invention the *piano e forte* (the Italian words for "soft and loud"), because it could sound notes with greater softness or loudness than a harpsichord. From this has come the modern

A beautiful old harpsichord, made in 1762. It has two keyboards, or manuals.

pianoforte, or piano for short. The most famous of all pianists was the Hungarian Franz Liszt. He was a very handsome and dashing man and women used to scream and faint when he played, just as though he were a pop star.

Organs are quite different keyboard instruments. They consist of pipes of varying shapes and sizes. As the organist presses down the keys, a current of air is admitted into the pipes, which sound notes of different pitch like a

A young pianist just starting his lessons. The modern piano is the successor to the harpsichord shown on the opposite page.

A modern church organ showing the arrangement of the pipes. The organist is using her feet as well as her hands.

wind instrument. One very old type of organ was called a "Bible" organ, because it was about the size of a large book and could easily be carried around. By contrast, there are giant organs, such as the one in the Royal Albert Hall in London, England, that has pipes as tall as a house. Large organs have several keyboards, including one made up of pedals, because there are many pipes to play. So an organist sometimes plays notes with his feet and his hands.

Electronic Instruments

We mentioned the electric guitar on page 11. Most electric guitars are made of plastic materials and look quite different from the traditional Spanish guitar. They sound different too, because their strings are wired up to electric loudspeakers. Instruments like these are known as electrically-amplified or electrically-aided instruments.

An open-air pop concert. Compare these electric guitars with the classical or Spanish guitars on page 11.

True electronic instruments are not modeled on any existing musical instrument. They make their own sounds without the aid of strings, wind in a pipe or tube, or any other long-established method. One such is the Hammond organ. Another is the Ondes Martenot, or "Martenot Waves," named after its French inventor, Maurice Martenot. In this case, electronic valves called **oscillators** create electric "waves," which are then made audible through a loudspeaker. The notes have a strange, unearthly sound.

A young player at the electric organ. Such instruments were once very popular in cinemas.

The "king" of electronic instruments is the synthesizer. An American inventor, Robert Moog, made one of the first. The word "synthesizer" means "building up," or "putting together." It has oscillators, and "mixers" and "filters," which combine the electric waves or modify them in some way, thus building up the sounds. A modern synthesizer can sound like a huge electronic orchestra – true music for the Space Age!

A modern synthesizer, showing all the different parts, including tapes and keyboard, that help to "build up" the sounds.

Glossary

Bow A rod with stretched horse hairs or strands of plastic, used for drawing across the strings of a violin or other similar instrument, to make the strings vibrate.

Embouchure French word describing the position of the lips on a wind instrument, or the actual mouthpiece on some wind instruments.

Frequency The scientific term for measuring the rate of vibrations in sound waves.

Key A small lever, part of the mechanism of a piano, organ and some wind instruments. In music, key also has a second, quite different meaning, connected with harmony.

Oscillator An electronic valve that changes electrical impulses or currents into "waves" or "patterns" of sound.

Pitch The precise degree of highness or lowness of a musical sound, directly related to the frequency of the sound waves.

Reed A small, thin strip (or strips) of wood or plastic inserted in the mouthpiece of some wind instruments, causing vibrations when blown upon. Some organ pipes also have reeds.

Sound waves Invisible waves or pulsations, caused by other vibrations, that travel through air (or water). When our ears pick them up, we hear them as sounds.

Tone The quality or "ring" of a musical sound, as distinct from its pitch. Each type of musical instrument has its own special tone.

Tuning Correcting the basic pitch of an instrument, so that it plays at precisely the same pitch as others.

Books to Read

American Indian Music and
Musical Instruments by George S.
    Fichter. McKay, 1978.
A Concise History of Music by
    Percy M. Young. David White
    Co., 1973.
The King of Instruments by
    Richard C. Greene. Carolrhoda
    Books, 1982.
Make Mine Music by Tom
    Walther. Little, Brown & Co.,
1981.
Musical Instruments You Can
Make by Phyllis Hayes. Franklin
    Watts, 1981.
See with your Ears: The Creative
Music Book by Don Kaplan.
    Lexikos, 1982.
Shining Brass: The Story of the
Trumpet and Other Brass by
    Daniel B. Tetzlaff, Lerner, 1963.

Picture acknowledgments
Mary Evans 5, 10; Sally and Richard Greenhill front cover and 25; Michael
Holford 24; Camilla Jessel 7; David Redfern 14; Sefton Photo Library 22, 23, 24;
Topham Picture Library 8, 15, 20, 28, 29; Zefa 6, 9, 11, 12, 13, 16, 17, 18, 19, 21,
26. Artwork on page 4 is by Mark Bergin.

Index

Bagpipes 18
Banjo 6
Bassoons 15
Boehm, Theodore 17
Brass wind instruments 12
Bugles 13

Cellos 9
Clappers 23
Clarinets 6, 15
Conch shells 4, 11, 12
Cornets 16
Cristofori, Bartolomeo 24

Double bass 6, 9
Drums 6, 20, 23

Electric guitars 27
Electric organ 28
Electronic instruments 27–9
Euphonium 16

Flutes 15

Gongs 21
Glockenspiel 23

Hammond organ 28
Harp 7
Harpsichord 24, 25
Horns 4, 12, 13

Jazz band 6, 14, 19, 23

Liszt, Franz 25

Military bands 16, 19

Oboes 5
Organs 25, 26

Paganini, Niccolo 10
Pan pipes 16, 17
Percussion instruments 20–28
Piano 6, 25
Pop groups 23, 27

Rattles 5, 23
Recorders 15

Sax, Adolphe 19
Saxaphone 14, 19
Spanish (classical) guitars 11, 27
Steel bands 21
Stringed instruments 7–11
Synthesizer 29

Tambourines 23
Triangles 23
Trombones 13, 14
Trumpets 6, 13, 14
Tubas 13, 16
Tubular bells 23

Violas 9
Violins 6, 8, 9

Wind instruments 12–19

Xylophones 22, 23